# SPIRITUAL
# MACHINERY

POCKET EDITION

Published from
Mardukite Borsippa HQ, San Luis Valley, Colorado
Mardukite Academy & Systemology Society
*for spiritual or educational purposes only*

# SPIRITUAL MACHINERY

## Systemology
## Professional Course
## Booklet #14

Developed by Joshua Free
for the Systemology Society

THE JOSHUA FREE IMPRINT
JFI PUBLICATIONS

Pocket Paperback Edition — *December 2023*

**mardukite.com**

# Chart Your Flight For Ascension...
## Then Let Your Spirit Fly!

Unlock your ultimate spiritual potential by removing barriers to your true native state.

Learn how to easily attain Self-actualization and help to actualize others along the way.

A greater appreciation and understanding of *Spiritual Life* and *Existence* awaits you. Expand your reach to achieve your dreams.

Each 'Professional Course' lesson-booklet offers simple exercises and techniques that directly apply the philosophy of Systemology, assisting to increase your true knowingness, improve your capabilities in this life, and even decide what you will do in your next.

At the Mardukite Academy of Systemology, the 'Professional Course' lessons in this series are presented to Seeker's that have already completed the 'Basic Course', previously released as six lesson-booklets, or the six-in-one single volume edition "Fundamentals of Systemology."

This all new presentation of the Systemology 'Pathway-to-Ascension' takes Seekers and continuing students from "Zero" to "Infinity" at lightning-fast speeds!

## Discover Who You Really Are...

## Because You Were Never Human

## Fundamentals of Systemology
Basic Course Lesson Booklet Series

#1 – *Being More Than Human*
#2 – *Realities In Agreement*
#3 – *Windows To Experience*
#4 – *Ancient Systemology*
#5 – *A History of Systemology*
#6 – *Systemology Processing*

## The Pathway to Ascension
Professional Course Lesson Booklet Series

#1 – *Increasing Awareness*
#2 – *Thought & Emotion*
#3 – *Clear Communication*
#4 – *Handling Humanity*
#5 – *Free Your Spirit*
#6 – *Escaping Spirit-Traps*
#7 – *Eliminating Barriers*
#8 – *Conquest of Illusion*
#9 – *Confronting the Past*
#10 – *Lifting the Veils*
#11 – *Spiritual Implants*
#12 – *Games and Universes*
#13 – *Spiritual Energy*
#14 – *Spiritual Machinery*
#15 – *The Arcs of Infinity*
#16 – *Alpha Thought*

# TABLET OF CONTENTS

## COURSE INTRODUCTION
- Welcome, Seeker! . . . 11
- A New View of the Human Spirit . . . 13
- Studying the Professional Course . . . 17
- Charting a Course on the Pathway . . . 22
- Taking Flight on the Pathway . . . 25

## LESSON FOURTEEN: SPIRITUAL MACHINERY
- Machinery and Circuitry . . . 33
- Some Basic Exercises . . . 38
- Facsimile-Copies: Machinery . . . 41
- Bodies: Physical & Otherwise . . . 47
- Handling "Bodies" . . . 55
- Further Toward Infinity . . . 66

## APPENDIX
- Glossary . . . 75
- Additional Resources . . . 93

# PROFESSIONAL COURSE INTRODUCTION

## WELCOME, SEEKER!
## LET'S CHART YOUR JOURNEY
## ON THE PATHWAY

*Systemology* is a "holistic" approach to understanding the human experience. It is not actually a singular "subject" in itself, but rather, a new way in which to view the many subjects of *Life* and all *Existence.*

This is a professional course in *Systemology*—specifically, how to *apply* the spiritual philosophy of *Mardukite Systemology* as a personal *"Pathway" to Ascension.* Our *Systemology* is a new approach to *"Self-Actualization."* It is completely relevant for the modern age and the future; and quite different from any previous similar attempts, or other traditions, you might find. What's more: it is applicable to anyone with any background.

This *"Professional Course"* series of lessons (booklets) immediately follows the material given in the *"Basic Course"* series — available as six separate pocket-sized booklets, or in a single hardcover volume titled: *"Fundamentals of Systemology: A New Thought For The 21st Century."*

This is a *new* presentation of *Systemology*, emphasizing the application of our philosophy for those *Seekers* that are *"Flying-Solo"* — or else working through their studies and exercises as solitary practitioners. This is a new innovation for *Systemology*. Aside from the book *"Crystal Clear,"* all of our former advanced courses have placed a focus on *"Traditional Piloting"* — where experienced practitioners assist *Seekers* in *"processing."*

To receive the greatest benefit from this study: it is expected that a *Seeker* will already be familiar with the fundamental concepts and terminology (previously relayed in the *Basic Course*) before using lessons from the *Professional Course*. This will allow us to cover the extensive territory of the *Pathway* much more quickly. However, for reference, a basic *"glossary"* of vocabulary used in this lesson is provided in the *"appendix."*

---

## A NEW VIEW OF THE HUMAN SPIRIT

*Systemology* is not a religion and does not require any type of *faith*. It is, however, built upon a "spiritual" premise—and as such is an "applied spiritual philosophy." It is based on ancient teachings that we are *Spiritual Beings* essentially "wearing" bodies like clothes—or using them as "vehicles." Yet our true native nature is not *physical,* but beyond this existence; and we can certainly operate a "body" from *outside* of it.

We are **all** *Spiritual Beings*—each of us a *unit* of *Spiritual Awareness*—that have experienced a very long *Spiritual Timeline* of existence. Although we might be particularly attached to the familiar "physical shells" associated with *this* lifetime, our true "*Spiritual Lifetime*" is seemingly *eternal*. We have been many things before *Human*, and we go onward as a *Spiritual Being* after our "*genetic vehicle*" of *this* incarnation perishes.

While a "spiritual" view of the *Human Condition* may not seem unique to our philosophy, just how often is the concept treated *systematically*? For that matter: just how many people, supposedly raised to this or that religion, or professing to believe one thing or another, actually live their lives as though they are *Spirits*?

As *Spiritual Beings* of immortal existence and infinite potential, we are not simply the "*creations*" of an even greater *Being-*

*ness*; we are, in fact, an integral part of that *"creative force"* which permeates all existence.

Our basic nature is to be a *"creative being"*—our highest goals are *"to create."* And as such a being—which we refer to as an *Alpha-Spirit* in *Systemology*—we have run into some difficulties along the course of our *Spiritual Timeline* and found ourselves trapped within material *Universes* of our own collaborative *creation*.

Since we did not start out our existence in a trapped condition, it is correct to say that we have *"fallen"* from our native *"godlike"* states. It did not happen all at one, but progressively and systematically. We know our "troubles" have resulted from accumulated "barriers" and "blockages"—or *fragmentation*—during our vast experiences as *Spiritual Beings*. They are not because we lack something; but because of what's been added.

In *Systemology*, we systematically examine those routes by which we must have descended to reach our present condition, then reverse the direction of travel and chart a personal *"Pathway to Ascension."* Of course, the exact "details" of the *Spiritual Timeline* will be different for each individual *Seeker*. However, we have been able to systematically chart our *Pathway* based on common patterns of *Human fragmentation*.

In the most basic terms: the *fragmentation* that defines our "downward spiral" consists of decisions or considerations where we deny our true nature. This includes those decisions to *"withdraw"* rather than *"reach"*; where we choose to *not-know* rather than *know*; to *not-communicate* rather than *communicate*; and ultimately, to take *no-responsibility* for being a *creative-cause*, and therefore succumb to being an *effect*.

16

But there is *hope!* And much more importantly: there is an effectively workable *way out* of the mazes and traps of our existence. If you are reading this now, you have already begun to gather your tools and build up the *"horsepower"* necessary to break the gravity holding your *Spiritual Beingness* to the *Human Condition.*

## STUDYING THE PROFESSIONAL COURSE

Most *Seekers* study and practice *Systemology* at-a-distance and independent of the "Mardukite Academy" or any "Master-level" mentors trained therein. This means that the *books* (and to a lesser degree, the *internet*) are the only means of direct contact a *Seeker* maintains with the "Systemology Society" during their studies. A continuing *Seeker* from the *"Basic Course"* will be familiar with the style of study found in *this* course.

Misunderstood words are the most common reason an individual abandons studying a subject. When a misunderstanding occurs, *Awareness* declines. These misunderstandings start to "stack up" after the first occurrence, and as a result, the level of interest and attention will also decline. This is how a "confusion" develops; and the individual will get "bored" with the subject, feel tired, and unable to concentrate.

One solution is to return to the part of the material that was still interesting and enjoyable to read. When scanning around that area of text, there is likely to be a new word (or new specific use of a familiar word) that is unclear, but was passed by unnoticed. All *Systemology* books include their own *glossary*. Using this *glossary* and a high-quality dictionary will help resolve this misunderstanding once it is located.

An effective education of any subject is taught on a *gradient*. This is what is intended by presenting the study of something as "*grades*." Rather than treating a subject as one total mass, true learning is achieved by increasing one's understanding with a *gradual* increase upward. The *ascent* to a mountaintop is not successfully achieved in one leap, but by targeting and reaching specific checkpoints along the way.

This *Professional Course* consists of a series of lessons (booklets) that gradually increase a *Seeker's* ability to understand and apply the practices and techniques of *Systemology* as a complete "*Pathway to Ascension*." It is an appropriate study for continuing *Seekers* (from the *Basic Course*), but also "advanced" *Systemologists*.

Each lesson (booklet) of the *Professional Course* applies *Systemology* to a particular subject (or focus). It is best if the entire course can be studied and applied in sequential order. These lessons also employ a style of practice or technique called *"Systematic Processing."* An introduction to applying this methodology is provided in the final lesson (booklet) of the *Basic Course*—or in the *"Fundamentals of Systemology"* volume.

To study the *Professional Course* just like a student at the Academy: a *Seeker* reads through all instructional material and applies each exercise (or *"process"*) presented in the text to the extent they comfortably can, before continuing on to the next lesson (booklet).

When first starting on the *Pathway* as a *Solo* practitioner, without the aid of an experienced *Pilot*, a *Seeker* shouldn't "push too hard" or allow themselves to get too "stuck" on any one area (lesson) or *process*. It is not expected that any one area will be completely handled when first introduced. For optimum results, it is expected that a serious *Seeker* will make more than one "pass" through the entire *Professional Course.*

The *Professional Course* is not altogether different from other forms of practical or technical education: where the instruction and exercises are delivered to a completion, and then a student further increases their abilities, strength and skill-level by applying additional practice throughout their life. Therefore, a student should not concern themselves with perfectly mastering each step (or lesson) before progressing forward.

Additional passes through the material are likely to result in different "*realizations*" (an increased *level of understanding*) than a previous time. New "layers" of *Knowingness* may now be accessible during a *process* that may not have been before. It is important to avoid invalidating the progress you've made just because one area is not completely handled right away, or if a certain *process* seems too difficult on the first pass.

## CHARTING A COURSE ON THE PATHWAY

Although we can communicate a systematic structure to *fragmentation,* the personal journey experienced along the *Pathway* will be different for each *Seeker.* For example, certain areas will seem more "*turbulent*" or difficult for one *Seeker* than another. We tend to say that these areas have more "*charge*" on them—or that they are more "*heavily charged.*" It is best to handle such areas when you are already feeling "good" and not in a situation (or condition) where that specific area is consistently being "*triggered*" or "*restimulated.*"

As an applied philosophy, *Systemology* "theory" can be easily utilized in the "laboratory" of the "world-at-large" in everyday life. This is implied within the basic instruction of each lesson. Unlike other "sciences" that conduct experiments by making a change to some "objective variable" *out there* and waiting to see an effect, our focus is the individual (or *Observer*) themselves, and how *they* affect the "*Reality*" perceived.

In addition to applying *Systemology* "New Thought" to everyday life, our philosophy is applied by using specific exercises and systematic techniques. These "*processes*" provide the most stable personal gain (and *realizations*) for each area; but only when actually applied with a *Seeker's* full "*presence*" and *Awareness*.

This *Professional Course* is designed so that it may be easily read and studied with little concern for what "dangers" these teachings—or *processing*—might unleash. However, there are still some guidelines that pertain to the "best-uses" of these course lessons, particularly if a *Seeker* intends for stable development.

Skipping over too much material/*processing* in early lessons may make attempts to understand (or apply) later lessons more difficult. However, once the complete *Professional Course* is worked through at least once in its entirety, specific areas can then be later returned to and treated with a greater sense of *Awareness* and *"presence"* than before. Of course, in *"Traditional Piloting,"* the rate of processing is monitored by an experienced practitioner; but in *"Solo-Processing,"* a *Seeker* must regulate their own progress on the *Pathway.*

Applying a systematic technique is called *"running a process."* The *processes* are designed with very simple instructions or *"command-lines."* To *run* a *processing command-line*, a *Seeker* may be assisted by the communication of that *line* from a *"Co-Pilot"* (as in *"Traditional Piloting"*). But even then, a *Seeker* must still personally "input" the *command* as *Self*. For this reason —and quite thankfully— *Solo-Processing* is possible.

## TAKING FLIGHT ON THE PATHWAY

*Processing Techniques* are intended to treat the *Spiritual Being* or *Alpha-Spirit*; the individual themselves. It is applied by the *Alpha-Spirit*—then *Self-directed* to the "Mind-System" or even a "body" (*genetic-vehicle*), both of which are "constructs" that the *Alpha-Spirit* (*Self*, or the "I-AM" *Awareness unit*) operates, but neither of which is actually *Self*. *Fragmentation* causes *Humans* to falsely identify *Self as* the *"Mind"* or even a *"Body."*

25

The *Professional Course* lessons (booklets) are designed for the *Beginning Seeker* in mind—one that may have an understanding of theory, but with little experience in practice. That being said: each of these lessons may be used toward total *Beta-Defragmentation* within a specific area. There are also more *processes* given for each subject than may be necessary to achieve an *ultimate end-point realization* on that entire area.

Some *processes* can be treated quite lightly at first; others may require a bit of working at in order to get "*running*" well. It is important to set aside a period of time when you can be dedicated to your studies and *processing.* This period of time is referred to as a "*processing session.*" The reason for this, is that when a *process* does start *running* well, it is important to be able to complete it to a satisfactory "*end-point.*"

The purpose of *systematic processing* is to be able to *really* "look" at things and even determine the *considerations* we have made—or attitudes we have decided—about *Reality* as a result of those experiences. It doesn't do us much good to simply "glance"—or to *restimulate* something uncomfortable and then quickly *withdraw* from it once again, leaving more of our *attention* yet again behind and held fixedly on it.

Generally speaking, a *Seeker* continues to *run* a *process* so long as something is "happening"—which is to say, the *process* is still producing a change. Usually this is evident by the type of "answers" that a *command-line* helps a *Seeker* originate from the database of their own *Mind-System*. The *command-lines* do not "do" anything on their own. They assist a *Seeker* to direct their own attention toward increasing *Awareness*.

Of course, a *Seeker* may also cease to generate new "data" from a *process* without reaching an *"ultimate" realization* as an *"end-point."* It is possible that additional "layers" (or even other "areas") require handling before anything "deeper" is accessible. If this is the case, end the *process.* But, if a *Seeker* is *withdrawing* from something uncomfortable that was incited or stirred up, then a *process* is *run* until they feel "good" about it.

In case the thought of encountering *"turbulence"* is a concern: the techniques given as *"Opening Procedures"* of a *Formal Session* (in the *Basic Course*), and those found in the earliest lessons of the *Professional Course*, are quite useful when applied as "safety nets" for maintaining *Awareness* and *presence*, even when *Flying-Solo.*

One of the benefits to *Flying-Solo* is that *processing* is entirely *Self-determined.* This already provides a certain built-in "safety" for a practitioner. Anything you *restimulate* by *Self-determinism* is *your thing*. It is not incited by external *other-determined* influences (or other "source-points" in existence) that make you an *effect*. It can be more easily handled in *processing*—or you can simply let things "cool down" and come back to it again.

While it may seem "mysterious" to beginners, a *Seeker* gets a sense for knowing how long to *run* a *process* only with practice. Once you have spent some time actually applying the *Professional Course*, there are many aspects that become "second nature" because they are, in fact, a part of our true original nature. All we have done is "*reverse engineer*" the routes of *creation* and *consideration* that are already *our own*.

# LESSON FOURTEEN: SPIRITUAL MACHINERY

# MACHINERY AND CIRCUITRY

In the previous lesson, we introduced the subject of *"energy"* and *"energetic systems."* Now, we advance this further by considering how *"matter"* (*forms*) and *"energy"* are combined to form *"machines"* and *"bodies."* By *"spiritual machinery,"* we mean mechanisms that are *"actual constructs"* carried by an *Alpha-Spirit* along their experience of *spiritual existence.* And, while they may not be *"physically apparent"* or perceived directly within the sensory range of *this Physical Universe*, they very much *exist* and *affect* us. A perfect example of this, is what is often referred to as a *"Mind."*

There are two main types of *spiritual machinery*. There is *light machinery* that is simply *created* as itself, as a *form* with a particular *function*; and there is *heavy machinery*, which is more "organic" in nat-

33

ure, because it is actually built out of *spiritual beings* (or else requires *an entity* be *entrapped within* it in order to function). For now, we will focus on *light machinery* as an introduction (leaving the subject of *entities* and *spiritual-identity fragments* for a more *advanced level* of personal development that follows *after* the *Professional Course*).

In basic terms, when we refer to *machinery*, we mean a *form* that is distinguished by its *programmed functions*. It *does* something; but it only *does* what it's *programmed to do*. In the case of our own "*Mind-System*," we mean a complex network of *energy-systems* that give the "*Mind*" its *form* and *function*. It is a vast array of "*circuitry*" that operates *automatically* on a "*push-button*" or "*stimulus-response*" basis.

The "*Mind*" is a *creation* of the *Alpha-Spirit* that continues to *persist* and is left to *create* for it *automatically*. The longer it *persists*, the more *"energetic-mass"* it seems to contain as a *form*, meaning the greater of a *"weight"* it becomes for our own continuing *spiritual existence. Traditional Piloting* requires communication with the *Alpha-Spirit*—the *actual individual*—and not some *social-machinery circuit* that when you ask *"how are you,"* it is *programmed* to automatically respond *"fine,"* even when the person is not. That is not *true communication.* This is why *actual presence in-session* is required for *systematic processing* to be effective.

*Upper-Level Systemology* is sometimes difficult for a *Seeker* to approach and understand without having already increased their *spiritual perception* (or *"ZU-Vision"*) with *Beta-Defragmentation*. Effectively working directly with these relatively "higher" areas requires more *actual intuition—Actualized Awareness.*

Starting with *Systemology Level-5* (*Lesson-11*), we began dealing more with *"things"*

35

(*terminals* and *forms*) and *"incidents"* that are not *directly* encountered (or typically *visible*) from *within* the normative "confines" or "limitations" of the *Human Condition*. Although they continue to affect our experience of *Beta-Existence*, they *perturb* and *impinge upon* our *reality* as an *"unseen source"* of various *creations* and *manifestations*.

In more *advanced* work, *"Biofeedback Devices"* may be used to detect when *fragmented charge* in certain *"unseen areas"* is present. So, what we are speaking of is not entirely "undetectable," just not always *knowingly* sensed, especially when it is *"active"* or *"restimulated."* [Our goal with the *Professional Course* is to take a *Seeker* as far as they can go *intuitively*, before introducing *advanced* applications of *GSR-Biofeedback, &tc.*]

There is nothing inherently wrong, or even *fragmenting*, about an *Alpha-Spirit* *knowingly creating spiritual machinery.* This is completely within the native abilities of *Alpha-Thought*. An individual can certainly make a *series of postulates* and *program* an *"external form"* to *automatically create* an *effect* when some *programmed* factor "triggers" or "activates" it—meaning, when something *"pushes the button"* so to speak. This is actually, in part, *how* we even started *creating Universes*; and then later, by *creating machinery* that could then *create* and automatically and invisibly *manage Universes.*

Much like any other *creations* and *"postulates"* an *Alpha-Spirit* makes: our troubles only come when we set our *creations* to *persist* (run forever), forget about them, and then lose all *responsibility* and *control* of them. This is essentially what *produces all* of our *fragmentation.* When an *Alpha-Spirit* fully regains *responsibility* and *control* of its own *creations*, it will also regain more of its own native *ability-to-create knowingly* once again.

Advanced philosophies aside, let's get busy doing some practical exercises for this lesson.

## SOME BASIC EXERCISES

A *Seeker* develops and applies their *visualization* and *mental imagery* skills all along the *Pathway*. At this *processing-level*, more and more of the exercises require that ability. A *Seeker* must be able to actually *get the sense* that they are *doing* something, or *creating* something, with their *intentions*—even in the absence of having a directly observable and solid manifestation.

We have practiced many exercises with the *Body's Eyes* closed, but here we will develop and apply the same principles with *eyes open*. One should work with this until there is a certainty on being able to clearly "superimpose" one's own *mental images* or *creations* "over" the *Universe* that is seen with the *Body's Eyes*. In previous lessons, we mainly use solid simple objects. Now we want to add some complexity to it. [There is also no expectancy for a "physically solid object" to suddenly materialize for others to see. That is not the intention; and what's more, there is no "postulate" made in this exercise for such to even occur.]

A. *"Look around (the room); Spot an object you like, which has a bit of complexity to it."*

B. *"Imagine (create/visualize) a duplicate-copy of the object right next to it."*

C. *"Alternate your attention between the two objects, one to the other; Spot any differences between the two and adjust your copy to more closely match the real one."*

Once a *Seeker* is fully confident doing this, the same exercise is practiced with *eyes closed*. However, this time, use *"ZU-*

*Vision*" (or "*Imagination*" if necessary) to "*Look*" around and "*Spot*" an object that is *outside* the room, preferably *outside* the building in which you're holding your *session*. If you're working outdoors already, put your *attention* on "*Looking*" at a *location* that is not close-by. Whatever it is you find to work with, make a *duplicate-copy* next to it and keep adjusting it until there are no noticeable differences.

Depending on a *Seeker's* previous development, it may require one or more *sessions* to be fully certain of ability with these two parts (above). For the final step, alternate between the two parts using different objects this time. With *eyes open*, pick an object in the room to *copy*; then with *eyes closed*, pick a large complex object that is *external* to the *room* (requiring a *viewpoint* that is "*remote*" from the *Body* in order to "*see*" it) and *copy* that. Then throw away or destroy all your copies and end the *process*.

The remainder of our basic techniques in this area (given in the next section) were first introduced to *advanced Seekers* many years ago in our original "*Wizard Training Regimen*" for *Systemology*.

## FACSIMILE-COPIES: MACHINERY

• Select an object that has the basic mechanical function: "*to produce a flow.*" [This may be initially practiced with a "sink" or "water-spigot" in the absence of a reality on *electricity* or understanding of *motion*.]

–With eyes open: *Look* at the mechanical object in the "OFF" condition; *Imagine* an identical duplicate beside it. *Look* between the two alternately; *Spot* any differences and adjust your *created-duplicate* to match the original. Continue until you're satisfied with the *certainty* of the *duplication*.

–Turn the mechanical object "ON"; *Look* at it in this condition, *noticing* the motion, and *getting a sense* of the *energy-flow* driving it. Adjust your *imagined duplicate-copy* to match this in every way.

–Then alternate these steps, *duplicating* the functions "OFF" and "ON."

• To advance this further: apply the previous steps, with eyes closed, using an object not present.

• Select a mechanical object that has a basic "motor" function. [An "electric fan" is best for practice until a *Seeker* has a greater reality on *generators* and *engines*.]

–Apply the basic steps (previously) for *imagining duplicate machinery*; this time *noticing* the internal mechanics: a *circuit* or *energy-flow* that drives or propels the *spinning-motion* of the *blades* that is *started* and *stopped* (*controlled*) with a *switch*. As it "runs" (is "ON") *get a sense* of the internal mechanics, matching this *energy* and *motion* in your *duplicate-copy*.

• For additional practice with the above steps: use more complex machinery; use machinery not present; use electronic devices. [A basic physical understanding of the way things work is quite beneficial. We recommend David Macaulay's *"The Way Things Work,"* which is illustrated and easy-to-understand.]

• With eyes closed: *Imagine Being* a *"motor-vehicle"; create* the machine, the internal mechanics, and *get the sense* of *"identifying with it"* as a *body*. Establish a *"point-of-view"* (POV/*viewpoint*) within the *vehicle*, while maintaining the *creation* and a *sense of* the *energy* and mechanical *motion* taking place inside of it.

–As an additional step: move your *point-of-view* through each of the *vehicle's* mechanical systems, while maintaining a *sense of* it running: steering, brakes, the engine, transmission, *&tc.*, to the extent of your reality on these systems. Even without previous knowledge, see if you can *get a sense* for how it operates *from the inside.*

In general, an individual will have many types of *"mental machinery"* active and running on automatic. In the following exercises, we simply want to *get a sense* for what some of that would be. After all, we either *created* it and forgot about it, or else we were *implanted* with it; but regardless its *ours* now—and it continues to *persist unknowingly* using our own *spiritual energy* as its *source*. This is not likely to be eliminated fully with this *Professional Course*, since its handling requires *advanced processing* used for *Alpha-Defragmentation*.

One setback to working with *mental imagery* and *spiritual energy* is the lack of "feedback" one gets from the *Physical Universe* to validate any gains in *spiritual perception* and *ability*. The following exercise "pretends" that we are *creating* and then simultaneously an *"uncreation"* occurs automatically, due to one of our *mental machines*. It's perfectly fine to treat this as a "theoretical" condition for this exercise without adopting it as a belief (prematurely to *knowing* it).

• *Imagine* (*create/visualize*) a large object, such as a piece of furniture, out in front of you. When you are satisfied with its form; *unmake* (*uncreate*) it. This doesn't mean keeping a *sense of it* there and just making it "invisible"; you apply the same level of *intention* you used to *make* it as *unmake* it. We practice by doing this *knowingly* and *intentionally*.

• *Imagine* that you have an "*unmaking machine*" above-and-behind one of your shoulders; that whenever you *make* the piece of furniture, the "*unmaking machine*" is making it "vanish" (*cease* to *exist*). Repeat this a few times with the same object. Then use different objects. Then do some more, but shifting the location of the "*unmaking machine*."

–Repeat the above step, but using a "*blackness machine*" (which overlays your *creation* with a "*cloud of blackness*").

–As before, but using an *"invisibility machine"* (turning your *creation "invisible"* when you make it).

• [Using the data above] *Imagine* (*create*) the furniture; use the *"invisibility machine"*; but this time, also *pretend* to *"Be"* a *"looking machine"* inside the *Body's Head*, which can *look through* the *invisibility* (and *see* the furniture anyway) and produce a *picture* or *mental image*.

–A *Seeker* practices the above step until they can do all parts as a single action: *knowingly creating* the object; *making it invisible* with one machine; *looking at it* as another machine; and ultimately *seeing* the *image picture* that the second machine produces. Then practice some more with different objects.

–Practice as before: using the *"blackness machine"* with the *"looking machine."*

• In a public place: *Look* around; *Spot* a "wall" or large object. *Spot* people; *Imagine* them having a *"reality machine"* that

46

projects the *reality* of the selected object/wall.

–As above; then *Imagine* that the "*reality machines*" also "*copy*" the *reality* from one person to the next (so that they all see the same *reality*).

–When a *Seeker* is comfortable with these steps, they can continue the exercise with different objects.

–Finally, practice this exercise on the "entire physical reality" that is viewable: *Imagining* that each person you *Spot* has a "*reality machine*" that projects the *reality*; and having each *machine copy* sent to the other "*reality machines*" (so that everyone is experiencing the same *reality*).

## BODIES: PHYSICAL & OTHERWISE

Systematically speaking, a *body* is a *symbol* that an *Alpha-Spirit* uses as their "*playing piece*" in a *game*. It is a "*terminal*" exist-

47

ing at a particular level of solidity or reality that is used to relay communication, perception and action. We often use the term *"genetic-vehicle"* to denote the organic *"Human Body,"* because obviously an *Alpha-Spirit* has used *other* forms as *"game tokens"* previously on their *Spiritual Timeline (Backtrack)*.

Earlier in our existence, we were able to simply *create* and *uncreate* *"bodies"* at *will* —or an *Alpha-Spirit* might leave a *"body"* in a known position so that others could contact it. In fact, even on Earth, there are reports from the ancient world about *"statues"* that *"gods"* once used to communicate from a distance. But early on the *Backtrack*, we did not *confuse* our actual *identity* as *"Self"* with these *token pieces*; and we had no difficulties or limitations in *creating* or *projecting* "bodily-forms" when we needed to.

As *games* became more interesting and more complex, we required more comp-

48

lex and restrictive *playing tokens* in order to participate. What began even as "simple objects" quickly evolved into more elaborate, dynamic and ever-changing *lifeforms* as *bodies*. At first, we still did not make the mistake of *confusing* "*Self*" with the *playing token* we were using. So, what happened?

• The next time you *play* a *board-game* (or *video-game*), *consider* how far "downscale" your *Awareness* would have to sink in order to forget that you were a *player* in a *game*, and actually believe that *you are* the *playing piece* that is being moved around, and even forget that what is happening is a *game*. What type of scenarios or sequence of events could bring this about?

We have all come down to this *Beta-Existence* through a long series of *Universes*; and each one involving the usage of specific *spiritual energy-systems* and *spiritual machinery*, each leading to more "*condensed*" (or relatively more *solid*) layers of

49

*"subtle," "etheric"* and *"astral"* bodies— and with each, adding a lower and lower *energy-center* to our *personal energy-system* (referred to commonly as *"chakras"* in the previous lesson).

Prior to *this Physical Universe*, the lowest denominator of *Beta-Existence* was the *"Magic Universe."* When *that Universe* was considered *"Beta,"* everything "above" it was *Alpha*. Once *this Physical Universe* came into being, then the *Magic Universe* became a part of *Alpha*. Everything shifts a level with each *Universe*.

In the *Magic Universe*, our lowest *"chakra,"* was near the level of *"genitals"* (what is now the second lowest). The lowest one that we now recognize today for the *Human Condition* (the *"rectum"*) was likely added during the transition from the *Magic Universe* in order to *anchor* the more *condensed* (*solid*) conception of a *"localized body"* that is used here in *this Physical Universe* now. The entire "*chakra*" system is solely designed to "*anchor*" the *viewpoint* of an *Alpha-Spirit* (as *Self*) to a "local" *body* that is in turn *anchored* to its own level of *Beta-Existence*.

• The next time you have access to some *game pieces, figurines,* and *dolls,* give yourself a chance to actually *play* with them. Just be *imaginative*; get the *pieces* interacting with one another; essentially do what a child might do with them.

– Select the *figurine* or *doll* you like best and *get a sense* of being *located inside* the "*doll*" (or whatever)—*seeing* from its *viewpoint, sensing* the *emotions, &tc.* Then, return to your original *viewpoint* as *yourself*; outside ("*exterior*") to the *game,* and "senior to" (or "above") it. Alternate: "*Being*" the *game piece/doll* and "*Being*" yourself.

This type of *play* is most effective as a practice if the *Seeker* is able to continue altering their *viewpoints* while manipulating the motion and interaction of the *pieces/figurines/dolls*. You physically continue to move the *"pieces"* around for the *game*, while alternating between your own *viewpoint* and that of the one selected *piece*. It may take some practice (several *sessions*) to comfortably shift *viewpoints* until you can reach a point of simultaneously being the *piece* and the *operator*.

One of a *Seeker's* goals for *Systemology Level-6* is to take this type of practice to an *end-point realization* where you can *perceive* or *recognize* this phenomenon taking place in the *Human Condition*; and to be able to maintain a *viewpoint* as an *Alpha-Spirit* (as *"senior"* or *"exterior"* to *Beta-Existence*), while simultaneously operating the *viewpoint* of the *"Human Body"* as your *"playing piece"* in *the Physical Universe Game*. It will likely require a second pass through the material of the *Professional Course* to get full *certainty/reality* on this.

• With eyes open; outside; in public: *Spot* a person that will be standing or sitting a while (such as at a bus-stop) so that you can practice the exercise without them leaving. *Imagine* (*create*) an identical *facsimile-copy* beside them. As with our earlier similar exercises: *look* at each alternately, *noticing* any differences and adjusting your *duplicate* to match. Then, *Spot* a different person and repeat.

–Additionally: if the person does leave your view during the practice, simply select another. If the person changes their position or location in the area, simply adjust your *duplicate* to match the motion.

–To advance this further: give particular *attention* to *copying* the internal parts of the *Human Body* (bones, organs, muscle, skin) and *get a sense* of the *organic-machinery* functioning inside (as with our previous exercises on *machinery* and *vehicles*).

–Finally: practice these steps to *create a*

*facsimile-copy* of a person in motion (*copying* the motion in your *duplicate*). *Get a sense* of how the internal *organic-machinery* is operating various "motor-centers" and "functions" during the motion. Practice this repeatedly on several different moving persons.

An additional practice would include applying these same exercises to "*animal bodies*" (for example, on a visit to a zoo). If a *Seeker* decides to do this, begin by making a "connection" with the *animals*. *Spot* them directly and silently acknowledge them for being there. *Get a sense* of them acknowledging you in return. It is best to practice with a few different *animals* to avoid *fixation imprinting*. Various potential *realizations* can also be gained by *Imagining* "Being" various *animal* forms (as a *secondary viewpoint* exercise).

## HANDLING "BODIES"

Another checkpoint of *Systemology Level-6* is for a *Seeker* to have some actual *spiritual perception* ("*ZU-Vision*") and an ability to *look* at their *Body* from a nearby *viewpoint* (that is *remote from*, or *exterior to*, it)—even if only vaguely. If this is not the case, then the exercises in this section are better left for your second pass through the course. Most of these exercises may be practiced with *eyes closed*.

NOTE: These exercises operate starting from a *viewpoint* that is *behind* the *Body*, *looking downward* at it.

• *Look* at the *Body* and *Imagine* (*create*) a *facsimile-copy* alongside it. This should be an identical *duplicate*; not a mirror-image opposite it. As other similar exercises: *notice* any difference and adjust your *copy*. Repeat this until you are comfortable with it.

–Then, as before: but reorient your *viewpoint* so that you are *looking downward* at the *Body* from a different position; do this for all relevant directions (from each side, from the front, from above and below).

–Then, repeat the above step, but changing the position of the *Body*: if you were sitting up, then practice it lying down, &tc.

• *Get a sense* that you are *behind* the *Body*, extending your *mental reach into* the *Body's Brain* using some kind of *energy-beam* in order to *control* it.

–Do this step (above) with *eyes open*; but still maintaining some *sense* of also *being behind* (or even to the *side* of) the *Body*, and *looking* at it as you *operate* it.

–Make a simple slow motion with your hand; *get a sense* for the *energy-flow* and *"nerve-impulses"* between the brain and the hand, causing it to move. Repeat several times, *noticing* how the *energy-flow* works. Repeat this step with your other hand a few times; then switch hands and do it again.

–Once you are comfortable with the previous step: start with the first hand, and as you perform the step, put your *attention* on *noticing* if you *get a sense* for any "*barriers*" or "*obstructions*" to a smooth *energy-flow* along the *channel* between the *brain* and *hand*. \*\*If you do: *Spot* two *points* just to either side of the *obstruction*, and using *intention,* gently *flow* some energy back and forth until it "*dissolves*" (or you don't *sense* it there anymore). [Anything you "*see*" is based on your *level* or *range* of acceptable *perception* and not likely to be exactly how these *energies* and *barriers* would "appear" if they were actually visible to normative senses.]

–Move the body some more in this wise and see if there are other "*barriers*" and "*obstructions*"; applying the technique (above) for "if you do."

An *Alpha-Spirit* has many *structural prog-*

*rams, energy-systems* and *mental mechanisms* hooked into a *genetic-vehicle (Body)* in *Beta-Existence.* We refer to it all as *"spiritual machinery"* because, while these things do not have any real material substance in *the Physical Universe,* they do have a material-like structure at an *Alpha* or *"spiritual"* (*"metaphysical"*) *level* of *Existence.*

On the *Standard Model* and *systemological charts,* we codify and systematize *seven-plus-one "levels"* between our experience of this *Beta-Existence* and our own native state as *Alpha-Spirit.* The sequence of *condensation* found in *"levels"* of *Universes* is actually mirrored in the *condensation* and *solidification* of *structures* and *machinery* that is actively at play.

Mystical models of *kabbalah* and *Star-Gates,* esoteric doctrines on *chakras* and *subtle bodies,* and various spiritual *books of the dead,* have all pointed toward a higher unified understanding of existence. It is unfortunate that the "*thinkingness*" of the *Human Mind* has prevented that true "incommunicable" and "unspeakable" unified understanding from unfolding for the initiates of *magical orders* and *mystical groups*.

Too often, the *mystic* and *magician* will become distracted by the pomp of classification and labeling. Unnecessary complexity, cultural flavors, and improper communication, all hinder the true personal development a *Seeker might* have gained from pursuing other routes. Many of the other possible avenues provided *some* progress; but when they eventually looped back to our original *Pathway*, we found that the detour was not a short-cut, but actually took longer to trek, and did not get us as far toward the goal after all. [This assumes a *Seeker* doesn't get lost altogether, early on, when chasing down these other paths.]

The "*Astral Body*" and the "*chakras*" originated with the *Magic Universe*—the next *level* "up" or "higher." It is these subjects that most *New Age* practices employ as an entry-point to "spiritual development"— without any *consideration* for the *steps* we've taken on our *Pathway* leading up to this point.

As a result, the *mystic* attempts to use their imperfect knowledge of these *energy-systems* as the total basis of a methodology toward *"Ascension."* The *magician* often goes one step further in assigning unnecessary *god-names*, *grimoire hierarchies*, and *mythological pantheons* to the process—further removing *Self* from *Cause*, and yet simultaneously thinking that all the superfluous data will somehow give them greater *control* of it all.

While we introduced our basic *systemology* of the *"chakras"* in the previous lesson, there is another *arcane energy-system* that originates from an ever *higher level* than the *Magic Universe*—and is therefore less "*condensed*" (*solid*) and easier to work with. Because this system consists of only "*golden orbs*"—and not a rainbow-array of fancy geometry (like the *chakras*)—it was likely easy to overlook among the many tears and surviving remnants of the most ancient esoteric lore on the planet.

Although the *chakra-system* is the most readily recognizable from contemporary metaphysical studies, we mentioned (in the previous lesson) that there were many other "*energy-centers*" or "*anchor-points*" in the body. While the *chakra-system* seems to mirror the "*ZU-Line*" and parallels the *central nervous system* of the *Human Body*, there are other *energy-centers* ("*golden orbs*") that are positioned, for example, near the joints and organs—and even a few (usually *eight*) key locations a couple feet *outside of* the *Body*.

To start with: the *three largest* "*golden-orbs*" are *in* the "*head*." They are "anchors" because they "track" with a *Body*.

They are not materially *inside* the *physical head* in *this Physical Universe*. They *exist* at the *level* that they originated; but they continue to "track" along with the *Alpha-Spirit* in the relative region of whatever it is *identifying* with for a *head*.

Since the *"Astral Body"* (from the *Magic Universe*) is formed quite closely to the "humanoid" form, it would seem that having a form with a *"head"* was preferable for a few past *Universes*. Prior to this, an *Alpha-Spirit* may have chosen just *"a golden orb"* itself, or even *"a nebulous cloud,"* as its *"contactable body"* (as would have been appropriate for much earlier *Universes*).

The structure of the *"golden-orb" system* is likely a couple *levels* (*Universes*) *"above"* the *Magic Universe* and the *"chakra"* system. We lightly introduce a *Seeker* to both *systems* only after earlier *processing levels*. Spending too much time (emphasis) on one or the other (or any) existing *struct-*

*ural energy-system* tends to increase an individual's *"reality-agreements"* with *that system*. This is why many *"New Agers"* get out of one "box" and find themselves in just a slightly larger more interesting "box" (but still in a *box*).

Much like how we handled the *chakras* (in the previous lesson), we will handle the *golden-orbs energy-system* by "approximation." The three *golden-orbs* in the *head* are the easiest to start with. They fit inside the *head* on a single plane next to each other, like *billiard balls* racked on a *pool table*. Although they are *"anchor points,"* we refer to them as *"orbs"* because (at least in the *head*) they "appear" much larger than a single *"point."* The ones at the critical joints (where the *Body* bends) are a bit smaller, as are the eight that are a couple feet outside the *Body*—and then there are also thousands of tiny ones throughout the whole system.

As with the *chakra-system*, handling the

*levels* of our *"personal energy-system"* can certainly make the *Body* "feel better" (and there are some other interesting effects that a *Seeker* may discover), but it is applied only after (or during later parts of) *Beta-Defragmentation procedures*, for additional "clean up" and "polishing."

A *Seeker* that worked with our *"chakra"* technique (in the previous lesson) will find this exercise easily workable. Again, we *Imagine* (*create*) lots of *"golden-orbs"* around area of the *Body* (such as the *head*). We don't put them inside the *Body* or apply any force to get them into a particular position. With *attention* on these *"anchor points"* specifically, as you place your *creations* in the vicinity, you should *get a sense* for where the "real ones" are, even if only vaguely. The idea is to intend for the "real ones" to *pull in* the *copies* you are *creating*. [For this exercise, *pushing in* with *force* may result in a *headache*.]

The *"golden-orb system"* originates from

64

earlier *Universes* on the *Backtrack* than even the *chakra-system*. Although it is designed to *persist*, its structure may seem even more decayed, discolored and misaligned than what is experienced with the *chakras*. But it may not. Some of the "repair" naturally occurs during *defragmentation processing*, but that alone doesn't always provide a *Seeker* the knowledge that these *systems* exist.

Similar to how we handled the *chakras*: as the *"anchors"* in the *head* become visible, they may not be very golden; so you can gently *flow energy into* them and get them back to their proper vibrant shining color. As with *"defragmenting energy-flows"* in other *systems*, you *free up* any "blockages" or *clear* any "dark spots" by *intending/creating* more *clear energy-flow* into the *system*. It's simply a matter of *controlling* the *system*—but this, of course, does not mean *"forcing"* anything.

The same principles apply if you *get a*

65

*sense* that these *golden-orbs* are "misaligned" (*out-of-position*)—and they most likely will be. Lightly add more *energy* and "encourage" them to shift back into their correct positions (without *pushing* or *applying force*). We handle these *systems* in this wise because it is the *systematic* approach. Since we cannot be absolutely certain of our *perception* of any of these "*higher-levels*," we may not know exactly where they are or where they should be. We handle it with *attention-energy*; just as we might apply *attention-effort* to turn "ON," "OFF" or "*change*" the functions of some other *mechanical system*.

## FURTHER TOWARD INFINITY

We often refer to *reactivity* as a *mechanism*, which is to say *machinery*. We refer to *response-mechanisms* and *defense-mechanisms*, and all kinds of *automatic reactive-mechan-*

66

*isms.* So, from the beginning, we even introduced our *systemology* of the "*Mind-System*"—or the nature of the "*Mind*"—as *spiritual machinery.*

Our *systematic processing* is actually quite easy to use, and is based on very few critical fundamental principles—but one of the most basic ones is: *get* a *Seeker* to *knowingly do* (or *create*) what they are already *doing (creating) unknowingly* as a means of putting it under greater *Self-Control* or *Self-Determinism.*

The supposed psychological authorities and ignorant critics of our techniques will argue that telling a person to do what they are already doing is a way to lay in manipulative control and brainwashing. And while they are *half-right,* these individuals are probably in most need of getting *processed* in this lifetime.

The truth is that, in *Traditional Piloting* we are *not* having a *Pilot* repeatedly comm-

67

and a *Seeker* to "sit in a chair" when the *Seeker* is already *sitting in a chair*. That would just be stupid. The technique in question is to have a *Seeker* knowingly as themselves (as *Self*) *get the sense* of *making* their *Body* "sit in the chair" as a preliminary step to greater *Self-Direction* and *Self-Determination*.

*Systematic Processing* requires that a *Seeker* put greater *attention* on making *deliberate actions* that are otherwise handled on *automation* and *stimulus-response*. This would be a "step up" for the kind of person that almost obliviously stumbles in and just plops down in a chair. Some beginning *Seekers* can barely *recall* much about how they got to our *office* before they are suddenly *present in-session*. It is obvious that many *fragmented* individuals are essentially *operating on auto-pilot*, to use an appropriate bit of slang.

That all being said, we will continue here with the next exercise without much additional explanation. Some of the underlying *"systemology"* here should now be more apparent to continuing *Seekers/students*.

• *Go around* the *room* and physically touch things; but as you touch each one, *Imagine* the *walls* yelling *"Mustn't Touch!"* at you; and then you let go (*withdraw*) very quickly.

–Eyes closed; repeat as above without moving around the room: this time *"mentally"* Spotting a thing; *reaching out* and *connecting* to it; having the *walls* yell *"Mustn't Touch!"*; and you rapidly *withdrawing*.

–Repeat each of the above versions (*physical* and *mental*): this time, when the *walls* yell *"Mustn't Touch,"* you ignore it (continue to touch the object) and decide when you want to let go (and then do so).

Often times when a *Seeker* has admitted to "not seeing anything" when they close their eyes (for example, in terms of "ZU-

*Vision*" or "*Recall*"), it is not because there isn't anything there, but it's been "blacked out." In more scientific language, this is called "*occlusion*" —which is from the same root-word from which we get "*occult*," which simply means "hidden from sight."

We like to say the phrase "out of sight is out of mind" —but unfortunately that is not the case, that is just how an *Alpha-Spirit* got a better *game*. These old programmed tendencies continue to carry with us as we take on more, and hence the continuing *condensation* and *solidification* of *Existence*. This next exercise is meant to provide better *recognition* or *control* of this "*blackness*" phenomenon by handling it *knowingly*.

• Eyes open: *Look* around the *room*; *Spot* an object; alternately (using *intention*) *push* a "*black energy-wave*" over the object (concealing it from your view) and *pull* the *wave* off it. Do this repeatedly a few times; then repeat this on a different object.

—Eyes closed; using the previous instructions: this time *Imagine* a large object, building or even an entire cityscape (or landscape); then *push* and *pull* the *wave* to conceal it from your view. Do this repeatedly for a single object/scene, then repeat it on another (preferably larger-scale) scene.

The final exercise for this lesson is directed at improving the quality of *"mental imagery"* that a *Seeker* can *create/visualize.* This is another area we introduce *after Beta-Defragmentation*—and for good reason. While still in a *highly fragmented* state, an individual has very little control over their *"reactive pictures"* and *"mental reactivity,"* so any premature efforts to make the quality of that *imagery* stronger also risks essentially making an individual worse. Obviously we don't want that to happen.

As an individual gains greater control over their *compulsively created machinery*, they can obviously do more with it *knowingly*, and perhaps even reach a point to dispense with it altogether (knowing full well that they could create it again at will). What we want to *exercise* in this technique is a *Seeker's ability* to literally *Imagine* an *"Infinity"* —and even demonstrate that it's not difficult to *conceive* of.

• *Imagine* (*create/visualize*) a light-gray *road* just suspended in empty space. From a *viewpoint* above it: *Look* down its *"length"* in one direction and *consider* that it is of *"infinite length"* and goes on forever. Move your *viewpoint* to *Look* in the other direction and extend that *"length"* *infinitely* that way too.

–Now (looking toward one of the directions) add (*create*) a *mile-marker* or *signpost* that says "0" on it, and place it beside the *road*. Move to a point you *consider* "one mile" down the *road* and add a *sign*

72

that says "1" on it. Go another "mile" and do the same (with a "2"). *Notice* that you could essentially keep on doing this "forever" given the *consideration* that the *road* is supposed to be *infinite*.

–Now add (*create*) a single *mental image* that displays these *sign-posts* on the side of the *road* extending out *infinitely*, making a *"postulate"* that each one is numbered "one higher" than the former. [The *signs* can all be the same, stretching out in the distance; you don't actually have to be able to see all the "numbers" at the same time.]

–Now *move to mile-marker "100"* and see it there. Then: *move to mile-marker "12000"* and see it there. Then: *move to mile-marker "6350"* and see it there. Finally: *move to mile-marker "0"* and see it there. Practice alternating a *move* (in *perspective/viewpoint*) to each of these different locations on the *road* and *notice* the numbered *sign-posts* as you do.

73

NOTE: If a *Seeker* finds difficulty with this: refer to the previous step; repeat the *"postulate"* (*intention* that something will *Be*) that there are *"infinite sign-posts"* until it "sticks" (so to speak).

—Try to end the exercise at *"mile-marker 0."* Then throw the whole scenery away; and repeat the exercise.

We will leave any *end-realizations* regarding this practice for a *Seeker* to discover for themselves. If something does *"resurface"* in the process; simply refer to the appropriate *lesson* from the *Professional Course* and handle it accordingly. By this point of the *Pathway,* you're farther than you think.

*The Systemology Professional Course*
continues in the next lesson booklet:
**THE ARCS OF INFINITY**

74

## GLOSSARY

**actualization** : to make actual, not just potential; to bring into full solid Reality; to realize fully in *Awareness* as a "thing."

**agreement (reality)** : unanimity of opinion of what is "thought" to be known; an accepted arrangement of how things are; things we consider as "real" or as an "is" of "reality"; a consensus of what is real as made by standard-issue (common) participants; what an individual contributes to or accepts as "real"; in *Systemology*, a synonym for "*reality.*"

**alpha** : the first, primary, basic, superior or beginning of some form; in *Systemology*, referring to the state of existence operating on spiritual archetypes and postulates, will and intention "exterior" to the low-level condensation and solidarity of energy and matter as the 'physical universe' (*beta*).

**alpha-spirit** : a "spiritual" *Life*-form; the "true" *Self* or I-AM; the *individual*; the spiritual (*alpha*) *Self* that is animating the (*beta*) physical body or "*genetic vehicle*" using a continuous *Lifeline* of spiritual ("*ZU*") energy; an individual spiritual (*alpha*) entity possessing no physical

75

mass or measurable waveform (motion) in the Physical Universe as itself, so it animates the (*beta*) physical body or "*genetic vehicle*" as a catalyst to experience *Self*-determined causality in effect within the *Physical Universe*; a singular unit or point of *Spiritual Awareness* that is *Aware* that it is *Aware*.

**alpha thought** : the highest spiritual *Self-determination* over creation and existence exercised by an Alpha-Spirit; the Alpha range of pure *Creative Ability* based on direct postulates and considerations of *Beingness*; spiritual qualities comparable to "thought" but originating in Alpha-existence, independently superior to a Mind-System.

**ascension** : actualized *Awareness* elevated to the point of true "spiritual existence" exterior to *beta existence*. An "Ascended Master" is one who has returned to an incarnation on Earth as an inherently *Enlightened One*, demonstrable in their words and actions; they have the ability to *Self-direct* the "Mind" and "Body" as *Self* (as a "Spirit"); and to maintain consciousness as a personal identity continuum with the same *Self-directed* control and communication of Will-Intention that is exercised, actualized and developed deliberately during one's present incarnation.

**associative knowledge** : significance or meaning of a facet or aspect assigned to (or considered to have) a direct relationship with another facet; to connect or relate ideas or facets of existence with one another; in traditional systems logic, an equivalency of significance or meaning between facets or sets that are grouped together, such as in $(a + b) + c = a + (b + c)$; in Systemology, erroneous associative knowledge is assignment of the same value to all facets or parts considered as related (even when they are not actually so), such as in $a = a, b = a, c = a$ and so forth without distinction.

**attention** : active use of *Awareness* toward a specific aspect or thing; the act of "attending" with the presence of *Self*; a direction of focus or concentration of *Awareness* along a particular channel or conduit or toward a particular terminal node or communication termination point; the Self-directed concentration of personal energy as a combination of observation, thought-waves and consideration; focused application of *Self-Directed Awareness*.

**awareness** : the highest sense of-and-as *Self* in knowing and being as I-AM (the *Alpha-Spirit*); the extent of beingness directed as a viewpoint (POV) experienced by *Self* as *Knowingness*.

**beta (awareness)** : all consciousness activity ("*Awareness*") in the "Physical Universe" (KI, in *Zuism*) or else in *beta-existence*; *Awareness* within the range of the *genetic-body*, including material thoughts, emotional responses and physical motors; personal *Awareness* of physical energy and physical matter moving through physical space and experienced as "time"; the *Awareness* held by *Self* that is restricted to an organic *Lifeform* or "*genetic vehicle*" in which it experiences causality in *beta-existence*.

**beta (existence)** : all manifestation in the "Physical Universe" (KI, in *Zuism*); the conditions of *Awareness* for the *Alpha-spirit* (*Self*) as a physical organic *Lifeform* or "*genetic vehicle*" in which it experiences causality in the *Physical Universe*.

**charge** : to fill or furnish with a quality; to supply with energy; to lay a command upon; in *Systemology*—to imbue with intention; to overspread with emotion; personal energy stores and significances entwined as fragmentation in mental images, reactive-response encoding and intellectual (and/or) programmed beliefs.

**channel** : a specific stream, course, current, direction or route; to form or cut a groove or ridge or otherwise guide along a specific course; a direct path; an artificial aqueduct created to connect two water bodies or water or make travel possible.

**circuit** : a circular path or loop; a closed-path within a system that allows a flow; a pattern or action or wave movement that follows a specific route or potential path only; in *Systemology*, "*communication processing*" pertaining to a specific *flow* of energy or information along a channel; "*feedback loop.*"

**communication** : successful transmission of information, data, energy (&tc.) along a message line, with a reception of feedback; an energetic flow of intention to cause an effect (or duplication) at a distance; the personal energy moved or acted upon by will or else 'selective directed attention'; the 'messenger action' used to transmit and receive energy across a medium; also relay of energy, a message or signal—or even locating a personal POV (viewpoint) for the Self—along the *ZU-line*.

**condense (condensation)** : the transition of vapor to liquid; denoting a change in state to a more substantial or solid condition; leading to a more compact or solid form.

**confront** : to come around in front of; to be in the presence of; to stand in front of, or in the face of; to meet "face-to-face" or "face-up-to"; additionally, in *Systemology*, to fully tolerate or acceptably withstand an encounter with a particular manifestation without an automatic reactive response.

**consideration** : careful analytical reflection of all aspects; deliberation; determining the significance of a "thing" in relation to similarity or dissimilarity to other "things"; evaluation of facts and importance of certain facts; thorough examination of all aspects related to, or important for, making a decision; the analysis of consequences and estimation of significance when making decisions; also in *Systemology*, the *postulate* or *Alpha-Thought* that defines the state of *beingness* for what something "*is.*"

**defragmentation** : the *reparation* of wholeness; collecting all dispersed parts to reform an original whole; a process of removing "*fragmentation*" in data or knowledge to provide a clear understanding; applying techniques and processes that promote a *holistic* interconnected *alpha* state, favoring observational *Awareness* of continuity in all spiritual and physical systems; in *Systemology*, a "*Seeker*" achieving actualized "*Self-Honest Awareness*" is said to be in a basic state of *beta-defragmentation*, whereas *Alpha-defragmentation* is the rehabilitation of the *creative ability*, managing the *Spiritual Timeline* and the POV of *Self* as Alpha-Spirit (I-AM).

**existence** : the *state* or fact of *apparent manifestation*; the resulting combination of the Principles of Manifestation: consciousness, motion and substance; continued *survival*; that which independently exists.

**exterior** : outside of; on the outside; in *Systemology*, we mean specifically the POV of *Self* that is *'outside of'* the *Human Condition,* free of the physical and mental trappings of the Physical Universe; a metahuman range of consideration; see also *'Zu-Vision'*.

**external** : a force coming from outside; information received from outside sources; in *Systemology*, the objective *'Physical Universe'* existence, or *beta-existence*, that the Physical Body or *genetic vehicle* is essentially *anchored* to for its considerations of locational space-time as a dimension or POV.

**fragmentation** : breaking into parts and scattering the pieces; the *fractioning* of wholeness or the *fracture* of a holistic interconnected *alpha* state, favoring observational *Awareness* of perceived connectivity between parts; *discontinuity*; separation of a totality into parts; in *Systemology*, a person outside of *Self-Honesty* is said to be operating from a *fragmented* state.

**flow** : movement across (or through) a channel (or conduit); a direction of active energetic motion, typically distinguished as either an *in-flow*, *out-flow* or *cross-flow*.

**genetic-vehicle** : a physical *Life*-form; the physical (*beta*) body that is animated/controlled by the (*Alpha*) *Spirit* using a continuous *Spiritual Lifeline* (ZU); a physical (*beta*) organic receptacle and catalyst for the (*Alpha*) *Self* to operate "causes" and experience "effects" within the *Physical Universe*.

**harmful-act** : a counter-survival mode of behavior or action (esp. that causes harm to one of more *Spheres of Existence*)—or—an overtly aggressive (hostile and/or destructive) action against an individual or any other *Sphere of Existence*; in *Utilitarian Systemology*—a short-sighted (serves fewest/lowest *Spheres of Existence*) intentional overtly harmful action to resolve a perceived problem; a revision of the rule for standard *Utilitarianism* for Systemology to distinguish actions which provide the least benefit to the least number of *Spheres of Existence*, or else the greatest harm to the greatest number of *Spheres of Existence*; in *moral philosophy*—an action which can be experienced by few and/or which one would not be willing to experience for themselves (*theft, slander, rape, &tc*); an iniquity or iniquitous act.

**hold-back** : withheld communications (esp. actions) such as "*Hold-Outs*"; intentional (or automatic) withdrawal (as opposed to reach); Self-restraint (which may eventually be enforced or

82

automated); not reaching, acting or expressing, when one should be; an ability that is now re-strained (on automatic) due to inability to with-hold it on Self-determinism alone.

**hold-outs** : in photography, the numerous snap-shots/pictures withheld from the final display or professional presentation of the event; withheld communications; in Utilitarian Systemology—energetic withdrawal and communication breaks with a "*terminal*" and its *Sphere of Existence* as a result of a "*Harmful-Act*"; unspoken or undis-covered (hidden, covert) actions that an indi-vidual withholds communications of, fearing punishment or endangerment of *Self-preserva-tion* (*First Sphere*); the act of hiding (or keeping hidden) the truth of a "*Harmful-Act*"; a refusal to communicate with a *Pilot*; also "*Hold-Back.*"

**holistic** : the examination of interconnected sys-tems as encompassing something greater than the *sum* of their "parts."

**Human Condition** : a standard default state of Human experience that is generally accepted to be the extent of its potential identity (*beingness*) —currently treated as *Homo Sapiens Sapiens,* but which is scheduled for replacement by *Homo Novus* (the "New Human").

**imagination** : ability to create *mental imagery* in one's Personal Universe at will and change or alter it as desired; the ability to create, change and dissolve mental images on command or as an act of will; to create a mental image or have associated imagery displayed (or "conjured") in the mind that may or may not be treated as real (or memory recall) and may or may not accurately duplicate objective reality; to employ *creative abilities* of the Spirit that are independent of reality agreements with beta-existence.

**imprint** : to strongly impress, stamp, mark (or outline) onto a softer 'impressible' substance; to mark with pressure onto a surface; in *Systemology*, used to indicate permanent Reality impressions marked by frequencies, energies or interactions experienced during periods of emotional distress, pain, unconsciousness, loss, enforcement, or something antagonistic to physical (personal) survival, all of which are are stored with other reactive response-mechanisms at lower-levels of *Awareness* as opposed to the active memory database and proactive processing center of the Mind; an experiential "memory-set" that may later resurface—be triggered or stimulated artificially—as Reality, of which similar responses will be engaged automatically; holographic-like imagery "stamped" onto consciousness as composed of energetic *facets* tied to the "snap-shot" of an experience.

**imprinting incident** : the first or original event

instance communicated and *emotionally en-coded* onto an individual's "*Spiritual Timeline*" (recorded memory from all lifetimes), which formed a permanent impression that is later used to mechanistically treat future contact on that channel; the first or original occurrence of some particular *facet* or mental image related to a certain type of *encoded response*, such as pain and discomfort, losses and victimization, and even the acts that we have taken against others along the *Spiritual Timeline* of our existence that caused them to also be *Imprinted*.

**intention** : directed application of Will; to in-tend (have "in Mind") or signify (give "signific-ance" to) for or toward a particular purpose; in *Systemology* (from the *Standard Model*)—the spiritual activity at WILL (5.0) directed by an *Alpha Spirit* (7.0); the application of WILL as "Cause" from a higher order of Alpha Thought and consideration (6.0).

**interior** : inside of; on the inside; in *Systemo-logy*, we mean specifically the POV of *Self* that is fixed to the *'internal' Human Condition,* in-cluding the *Reactive Control Center* (RCC) and Mind-System or *Master Control Center* (MCC); within *beta-existence*.

**internal** : a force coming from inside; informa-tion received from inside sources; in *Systemo-logy*, the objective experience of *beta-existence*

85

associated with the Physical Body or *genetic vehicle* and its POV regarding sensation and perception; from inside the body; in the body.

**invalidate** : decrease the level or degree or *agreement* as Reality.

**mental image** : a subjectively experienced "picture" created and imagined into being by the Alpha-Spirit (or at lower levels, one of its automated mechanisms) that includes all perceptible *facets* of totally immersive scene, which may be forms originated by an individual, or a "facsimile-copy" ("snap-shot") of something seen or encountered; a duplication of wave-forms in one's Personal Universe as a "picture" that mirror an "external" Universe experience, such as an *Imprint*.

**perception** : internalized processing of data received by the *senses*; to become *Aware of* via the senses.

**pilot** : a professional steersman responsible for healthy functional operation of a ship toward a specific destination; in *Systemology*, an intensive trained individual qualified to specially apply *Systemology Processing* to assist other *Seekers* on the *Pathway*.

**point-of-view (POV)** : a point to view from; an opinion or attitude as expressed from a specific identity-phase; a specific standpoint or vantage-point; a definitive manner of consideration specific to an individual phase or identity; a place or position affording a specific view or vantage; circumstances and programming of an individual that is conducive to a particular response, consideration or belief-set (paradigm); a position (consideration) or place (location) that provides a specific view or perspective (subjective) on experience (of the objective).

**postulate** : to put forward as truth; to suggest or assume an existence *to be*; to state or affirm the existence of particular conditions; to provide a basis of reasoning and belief; a basic theory accepted as fact; in *Systemology*, Alpha-Thought —the top-most decisions or considerations made by the Alpha-Spirit regarding the "*isness*" (what things "are") about energy-matter and space-time.

**presence** : a quality of some thing (*energy/matter*) being "present" in space-time; personal orientation of *Self* as an *Awareness* (*POV*) located in present space-time (environment) and communicating with extant energy-matter.

**processing command line (PCL)** : a directed input; a specific command using highly selective language for *Systemology Processing*; a predetermined directive statement (cause) intended to focus concentrated attention (effect).

**processing, systematic** : the inner-workings or "through-put" result of systems; in *Systemology*, a method of applied spiritual technology used toward personal Self-Actualization; methods of selective directed attention, communicated language and associative imagery that increases personal control of the human condition.

**realization** : the clear perception of an understanding; a consideration or understanding on what is "actual"; to make "real" or give "reality" to so as to grant a property of "being-ness" or "being as it is"; the state or instance of coming to an *Awareness*; in *Systemology*, "gnosis" or true knowledge achieved during *systematic processing*; achievement of a new (or higher) cognition, true knowledge or perception of Self; a consideration of reality or assignment of meaning.

**responsibility** : the *ability* to *respond*; the extent of mobilizing *power* and *understanding* an individual maintains as *Awareness* to enact *change*; the proactive ability to *Self-direct* and make decisions independent of an outside authority.

**Seeker** : an individual on the *Pathway to Self-Honesty*; a practitioner of *Mardukite Systemology* or *Systemology Processing*, that is working toward *Spiritual Ascension*.

**Self-actualization** : bringing the full potential of the Human spirit into Reality; expressing full capabilities and creativeness of the *Alpha-Spirit*.

**Self-determinism** : the freedom to act, clear of external control or influence; the personal control of Will to direct intention.

**Self-honesty** : the basic or original *alpha* state of *being* and *knowing*; clear and present total *Awareness* of-and-as *Self*, in its most basic and true proactive expression of itself as *Spirit* or *I-AM*—free of artificial attachments, perceptive filters and other emotionally-reactive or mentally-conditioned programming imposed on the human condition by the systematized physical world; the ability to experience existence without judgment.

**spiritual timeline** : a continuous stream of moment-to-moment *Mental Images* (or a record of experiences) that defines the "past" of a spiritual being (or *Alpha-Spirit*) and which includes impressions (*imprints, &tc.*) from all life-incarnations and significant spiritual events the being has encountered; in Systemology, also "*backtrack.*"

**Spheres of Existence** : a series of *eight* concentric circles, rings or spheres (each larger than the former) that is overlaid onto the Standard Model of Beta-Existence to demonstrate the dynamic systems of existence extending out from the POV of Self (often as a "body") at the *First Sphere*; these are given in the basic eightfold systems as: *Self, Home/Family, Groups, Humanity, Life on Earth, Physical Universe, Spiritual Universe* and *Infinity-Divinity.*

**Systemology** : a modern tradition of applied religious philosophy and spiritual technology based on *Arcane Tablets* (in combination with "*general systemology*" and "*games theory*") developed in the New Age underground by Joshua Free in 2011 as an advanced futurist extension of the *Mardukite Research Org.*

**terminal (node)** : a point, end, or mass, on a line; a connection point for closing an electric circuit, such as a post on a battery terminating at each end of its own systematic function; a point of connectivity with other points; in systems, a contact point of interaction; a point of interaction with other points.

**turbulence** : a quality or state of distortion or disturbance that creates irregularity of a flow or pattern; the quality or state of aberration on a line (such as ragged edges) or the emotional "turbulent feelings" attached to a particular flow or terminal node; a violent, haphazard or disharmonious commotion (such as in the ebb of gusts and lulls of wind action).

**validation** : a reinforcement of agreements or considerations as being "real."

**viewpoint** : see *"point-of-view" (POV)*.

**willingness** : the state of conscious Self-determined ability and interest (directed attention) to *Be, Do* or *Have*; a Self-determined consideration to reach, face up to (*confront*) or manage some "mass" or energy; the extent to which an individual considers themselves able to participate, act or communicate along some line, to put attention or intention on the line, or to produce (create) an effect.

*ZU* : the ancient Sumerian cuneiform sign for the archaic verb—*"to know," "knowingness"* or *"awareness"*; in *Mardukite Zuism and Systemology*, the active energy/matter of the "Spiritual Universe" (AN) experienced as a *Lifeforce* or *consciousness* that imbues living forms extant in the "Physical Universe" (KI); *"Spiritual Life Energy"*; energy demonstrated by the WILL of an actualized *Alpha-Spirit* in the "Spiritual Universe" (AN), which impinges its *Awareness* into the Physical Universe (KI), animating/controlling *Life* for its experience of *beta-existence* along an individual Alpha-Spirit's personal *Identity-continuum*, called a *ZU-line*.

*Zu*-**Line** : a theoretical construct in *Mardukite Zuism and Systemology* demonstrating *Spiritual*

91

*Life Energy (ZU)* as a personal individual "continuum" of Awareness interacting with all Spheres of Existence on the Standard Model of Systemology; a spectrum of potential variations and interactions of a monistic continuum or singular *Spiritual Life Energy* demonstrated on the Standard Model; an energetic channel of potential POV and "locations" of Beingness, demonstrated in early Systemology materials as an individual Alpha-Spirit's personal *Identity- continuum*, potentially connecting *Awareness* of *Self* with "*Infinity*" simultaneous with all points considered in existence; a symbolic demonstration of the "*Life-line*" on which *Awareness (ZU)* extends from the direction of the "Spiritual Universe" (AN) in its true original *alpha state* through an entire possible range of activity resulting in its *beta state* and control of a *genetic-entity* occupying the *Physical Universe (KI)*.

**Zu-Vision** : the true and basic (*Alpha*) Point-of-View (perspective, POV) maintained by *Self* as *Alpha-Spirit* outside boundaries or considerations of the *Human Condition* and *exterior* to beta-existence reality agreements with the Physical Universe; a POV of Self *as* "a unit of Spiritual Awareness" that exists independent of a "body" and entrapment in a *Human Condition*; "spirit vision" in its truest sense.

*explore the*
## Fundamentals of Systemology

All *six*
Basic Course
lesson booklets
*in one*
hardcover
edition!

*start your journey on the*
## The Pathway to Ascension

All *sixteen*
Professional Course
lesson booklets
*in two*
hardcover
volumes!

# THE SYSTEMOL

Seekers and students of the *Basic Course* and *Professional Course* will also be interested in the *Systemology Core Research Series*. These eight volumes are a complete chronological record of the Mardukite New Thought developments from the Systemology Society, published in 2019 through 2023.

The *Systemology Core* begins with the first professional publication released when the *Mardukite Systemology Society* emerged from the underground in 2019, with: "*The Tablets of Destiny Revelation.*"

# OGY PATHWAY

The Tablets of Destiny Revelation:
*How Long-Lost Anunnaki Wisdom
Can Change the Fate of Humanity*

Crystal Clear: *Handbook for Seekers*

Metahuman Destinations (*2 volumes*)

Imaginomicon:
*Approaching Gateways to Higher Universes*

Way of the Wizard: *Utilitarian Systemology*

Systemology-180: *Fast-Track to Ascension*

Systemology Backtrack:
*Reclaiming Spiritual Power & Past-Life Memory*

PUBLISHED BY THE **JOSHUA FREE** IMPRINT REPRESENTING

**The Mardukite Academy of Systemology**

**mardukite.com**